I am grateful for the gift of reading this amazing sojourn of a strong woman dedicated to her spiritual path. This is a must-read for any student entering the spiritual practitioner path.

Joanie McMenamin has taken berth, walking strongly and embracing her dedication to living spiritual principles. She demonstrates the principles of love, wisdom, and service.

Joanie's excellent writing skills enable her to capture her journey for readers. She shares from her heart the many turns on her path that provide to her the evidence of the presence of Spirit at every bend in the road.

You will find evidence of the waves of spiritual presence that continue reminding her of the inner cosmic compass. From this walk of strength and conviction, she steps into the ocean of Love-Intelligence to serve others with her deep conviction of the presence of the sacred Spirit, which is the God presence in all.

–Dr. Rev. Patty Luckenbaugh, D.D.,
Associate Minister, Prayer and Care Ministry,
Mile Hi Church, Lakewood, Colorado;
Author of *I Only Walk On Water When It Rains*

Joanie McMenamin has written a powerful story about the unfolding of spiritual awakening in *My Life As Prayer*. Beginning this journey through the eyes of a child and feeling the intense calling to recognize humanity's oneness, she is able to encapsulate the awe in deeply knowing this presence.

She uses humor to capture the magnificent through the mundane and see Spirit in the eyes of the lost. *My Life As Prayer* is an outstanding application of Science of Mind Treatment to the events of one's life and can be used as a practitioner primer. It will also be an inspirational and thought-provoking read for anyone examining their spirituality or doing a life review.

This book includes prayers and affirmations throughout to allow readers time to pause and reflect on their own experiences. *My Life As Prayer* is the first published book by this talented author and shows the reader the great potential she has for many more profound narratives.

—Bree Steldt, M.S.N., R.N., H.N.B.-B.C.

My Life as Prayer

Joanie McMenamin

My Life as Prayer

Joanie McMenamin

Park Point
PRESS

Park Point Press is an imprint of Centers for Spiritual Living
573 Park Point Drive | Golden CO 80401

My Life As Prayer
Copyright © 2022 Joanie McMenamin
All rights reserved.

No part of this book may be reproduced in any form without permission in writing from the publisher, except for brief quotations embodied in critical articles or reviews

Park Point
PRESS

573 Park Point Drive
Golden, CO 80401-7402
720-496-1370
www.csl.org/publications/books
www.scienceofmind.com/publish-your-book
Printed in the United States of America
Published 2022
Editor: Julie Mierau, JM Wordsmith
Design/Layout: Steffani Pitzen

ISBN paperback: 978-1-956198-22-5

ISBN ebook: 978-1-956198-23-2

Dedication

I dedicate this book to my youngest sister, Susie McMenamin (1973-2021), the most courageous warrior I know. She graced my life and let me know how loved I was from 2,000 miles away. Bless you, Suz, for showing me all I needed to know about life in two hours and allowing me to walk you home that evening.

Contents

Acknowledgments xi
Disclaimer xiii
Editor's Note xv
Introduction 1
    Who Am I? 2
    My Purpose 3
    How to Use this Book 3
    Starting Your Journey 5

Chapter 1: Hearing a Song that Has Not Been Sung Before 7
    Start with Recognition 9
    The Summer of 1977 9
    The Child Who Finds Spirit 11
    The Epiphany 12
    The First Tithe and Prayer 13
    Thinking of that Moment 14
    Reflections 16
    A Prayer of Recognition 17

Chapter 2: Greeting Presence By Name 19
    Taking the Next Step 21
    The 1980s and the Challenges that Came Forward 21

Self-Discovery at a Thrift Store   23
The Night Shift   24
Prelude to a Chance Encounter   25
The Eyes of a Lost Soul   26
The Escape   28
Reflections   29
A Prayer of Unification   31

Chapter 3: Walking a Path Unknown 33
Finding the Spiritual Truth   35
Meeting Dolly   36
The Clean Up   37
Putting Things Away   39
Dolly and the Realization   40
Reflections   41
A Prayer of Realization   42

Chapter 4: Gifts, Blessings, and Other Miscellanea 45
Appreciation of Life's Offerings   47
Finding Grace   48
Coming Home, Again   49
Opening to a New Path   50
Reflections   51
A Prayer of Thanksgiving   53

Chapter 5: Where to From Here? 55
Learning to Let Go   57
Flashback to 1984   58
The Journey Begins   59
Reflection   61
A Prayer of Release   61

References   67
Author Bio   69

Acknowledgments

My deepest and most heartfelt acknowledgment to the ministry of Mile Hi Church: Dr. Michelle Medrano, Rev. Josh Reeves, Rev. Carol Wilke, Dr. Patty Luckenbaugh, Dr. Barry Ebert, Rev. Jackie Harris, Rev. Michelle Scavetta, Rev. Simon Shadowlight, Rev. Zemirah Jazwierska, Rev. Millie Forsberg, Rev. Nadine Cox. Your presence in my life will always humble me. Thank you!

I give only my most profound appreciation to all my instructors, my teaching assistants, and my practitioners who guided me on this journey. It is my delight to grace the practitioners I met with over these two years with these words: You taught me to pray, to believe, and to become. It is my gift of fulfillment to my Practitioner Class of 2022 at Mile Hi Church, dubbed the Sacred Soul Sisters, with whom I walked every day on this path for two years. It is a love song sung out of key and with pure joy.

Thank you to Jennie Page, Bree Steldt, and Stephanie Finne for your eagle eyes and reviews for this effort. Ladies, I bow to you. Thank you so much! I am grateful and blessed to have Julie Mierau, Steff Pitzen, Kari Johnson, Holli Sharp, Stephanie Finne and everyone at Park Point Press assisting me with the manuscript

My Life as Prayer

and publishing efforts. I appreciate your care and wonderful guidance in the process to bring forward this book. Blessings!

To Dr. Roger Teel, bless you, sir, for being the first light on my path. To Erica Teel, R.Sc.P., that was one heck of a blessing you bestowed on me. Thank you!

Disclaimer

This book is a memoir. It reflects the author's recollections of experiences over time. Names and characteristics of individuals have been changed to respect their privacy; events and geographical locations have been compressed; dialogue has been recreated. The events and stories in this book are presented here to the best of the author's recollection and are meant to illustrate the context of the materials as part of an instructional overview.

– Joanie McMenamin, Author

Editor's Note

Many names for God appear in this book—Spirit, Source, Life, Love, Creative Intelligence, among others. All synonyms for God are set off with initial capital letters.

Throughout this work, as in other New Thought texts, references to Religious Science and to Science of Mind (or the Science of Mind) use the terms interchangeably. These terms refer to a philosophy and belief system, founded by Ernest Holmes more than 100 years ago, that today operates under the auspices of Centers for Spiritual Living (CSL).

— Julie Mierau, Editor

Introduction

This is a personal journey spanning fifty years, from the East Coast to the Hawaiian Islands, to a puddle in a pasture, to that moment of thanking Spirit for all of it. Life is an affirmative prayer that keeps growing and building in its magnificence, as much as we grow and expand abundantly in who we are as children of God.

When I experienced this spiritual awakening, I did not know about New Thought or metaphysics. Years later, I became familiar with a book called *The Science of Mind*, the teachings of Ernest Holmes.

As the founder of Religious Science, Holmes notes that our recognition of nature, be it as literal as leaves in the wind or birds that take flight, is the recognition of Spirit. When we tie into that greatness around us, we feel, know, and experience what we call by many names. When we hear our song—the call, the truth within us—we recognize this nature. It is preeminent and omniscient. It is the rapture that captures our hearts (Holmes, *The Science of Mind*, p. 130.3).

May we become enlightened to this call in our practice and sing to others our songs of beauty in the teachings we know from Holmes and the religions of our world. May our uniqueness be the sweetness others seek, the calm in the storms others face, and may our words bring forward the greatness in prayer as the healing for others becomes known.

Who Am I?

I am the daughter of an airline mechanic and a bank teller, an independent woman who grew up in humble surroundings filled with events that challenged me to grow stronger and more loving each and every day. I am someone who dared to be myself at a time in American history that is now unfolding again before us. As my life evolved, my faith and appreciation of God, as I understood God to be, grew, alongside the communities I lived in, bringing me forward to becoming a licensed practitioner in my church.

My practitioner journey began in September 2004 when I took Science of Mind 101 (now called Beyond Limits) with Dr. Roger Teel at Mile Hi Church in Lakewood, Colorado. Life has a funny way of changing things, and I found myself vested deeply in my own healing, self-discovery, and other personal adventures shortly after I took the class. After a twelve-year sojourn away from Religious Science, I returned to Mile Hi Church in 2016 and started to realize the importance of the teachings of Ernest Holmes in my time away from the church. I decided to pick up where I left off on the practitioner path in the summer of 2019. I received my stole and the honor of being a licensed prayer practitioner with the Centers of Spiritual Living at Mile Hi Church in the summer of 2022.

I know for myself that all that has happened is the grace and the blessings I deserve. I am that girl. I am that soldier. I am that cowgirl. I declare these to be so, and I earned every bit of the lessons learned to bring me forward in this truth, this knowingness, in the fullness of the thanksgiving I celebrate now, with only my faith exemplified and my worthiness laid bare to all. In all that has come forward, the essence of the seed I planted has grown to be magnificent. The fruits of my harvest in my life's experience are the bounty I share with all the other people who, like me, wonder where did it all come from. Frankly, Life seems it came out of nowhere, It got me to this appreciation, and I thank Life for it all.

My Purpose

My motivation for writing this book is to bring love, light, and joy to the experience of becoming a practitioner through an analogy of my life and the five steps of prayer. This is for anyone at any level of knowledge or desire or possible vested interest—if only slightly. It is to open the hearts and minds of all who seek to enter into the vast, incredible, endless, and fulfilling journey of spiritual practice.

All Spiritual Mind Treatments are predicated on a purpose for prayer. For this book, that purpose is to know fully the recognition, unification, realization, thanksgiving, and release that all that Life holds is wonderful, mysterious, messy, grand, and blessed.

How to Use This Book

Each chapter of this book reflects on one of the five steps of affirmative prayer, also called Spiritual Mind Treatment. I begin each chapter with a moment from my life that relates to that step and then reflect on how I came to find my prayer of affirmation because of it.

Outlined here are the five steps of affirmative prayer, as practiced by Religious Scientists.

Recognition

In the first step of affirmative prayer, we recognize that Spirit is all things of nature. The first chapter of a spiritual seeker's life is the unexplained feeling of love in the form of agape, by which I mean the unexplained feeling of love for all things. It evolves into the knowingness of self and Self; it becomes Its composition.

I heard my song as a child while becoming a woman along the Delaware shoreline near a town called Rehoboth Beach. You may listen to your song in the Rocky Mountains outside of Denver, on the Great Plains in Nebraska or Kansas, along a river in Iowa or Missouri, or beside the Great Salt Lake in Utah. Maybe it is not a cosmic tune of the universe for you? Still, a vista of Big Sur in California or Cannon Beach along the Oregon Coast, the orchards in Ohio or Michigan, and a covered bridge in New England could be images that brought you to know yourself and the spirit of that place.

Unification
In unification, the second step of affirmative prayer, we see what Ernest Homes describes as self and Self. The smaller individual self is a part of the larger collective "Self," referred to as Spirit or God. The two together are One (*The Science of Mind*, Holmes, p. 444.1). I am self, the smaller, Spirit is Self, the more significant, and when the two are One, there is no smaller or larger. Unification becomes the whole of the Universe, the Cosmic Consciousness, the Oneness, and where the power of prayer accelerates into the whole of the realization of healing, manifestation, and affirmation. In this unification, the complete union of knowing I am a child of God, that God is and I am, the power of the prayer pulls together in One.

Realization
Moving from the recognition of the beauty of God to the connection we all have with God as One, the third part of affirmative prayer is where realization unfolds the truth of being into a declaration. This is the most profound and most enlightening part of the affirmative prayer: We enter into the truth and the know-

Introduction

ing of everything and all things. We come to realize the beauty of God in ourselves, the truth we know as fact, not the experiences that drive us to believe in what the world is influencing us to be.

Thanksgiving
The fourth part of the affirmative prayer is the thanksgiving we bring to our recognition, unity, and realization of all truth and blessings we know of ourselves and others. It is short and sweet; it lifts us to the abundance and manifestation of all good things and the Good Itself. Sometimes we pause gently at this moment and allow the silence to expand the appreciation of the time we have given to our prayer. Then we take this gift of thanks and move to the final step and release it.

Release
One phrase I use in all of my prayers, especially in the fifth part of the prayer, is that I release my word into the Law. The Law is the Law of God. In the teachings of Religious Science, it is Universal Law, the all-encompassing mandate that fulfills the prayer as it is given. How prayer is served, it is given ideally.

Starting Your Journey

We all become seekers in many ways, along many paths, from many places, and so often, we are who we are from our journeys through our choices. We are all novices as we start our day; we are enlightened as we close our eyes and rest for the night. As I progress through this book, take my hand, and we will explore this spiritual seeking life together. No one walks independently. We each need someone willing to take that walk with us. Spirit is ready to take your hand anytime and walk with you, run with you, dance with you.

There are prayers at the end of each chapter you can use or adapt to meet your needs in understanding each one of the five

My Life as Prayer

steps. They are brief and meant to encourage you to expand on them in ways that you know for yourself, to see the best ways prayer works in your life. Each step is noted as well to help in identifying the breaks where each part comes into the prayer. I encourage journaling and writing out prayers. Please use these suggestions or prompts in crafting your own personal expression of divinity and love.

I am here to pray with you. This is the affirmative prayer of my life. Let's pray together.

Chapter 1

Hearing a Song that Has Not Been Sung Before

Recognition: God Is All There Is

There is one nature diffused through all nature;
One God incarnated in all peoples.

—Ernest Holmes, *The Science of Mind,* pg. 42

Start With Recognition
The first chapter of a spiritual seeker's life is the unexplained feeling of love in the form of agape, by which I mean an overarching feeling of love for all things. It evolves into the knowingness of self and Self; it becomes its composition. Knowing yourself is a tremendous advance in growth. Overcoming the challenges you face brings you to experience your soul.

You may have grown through a twelve-step program, a caring therapist or group who looked for your best to come forward, or a medical condition that brought about a knowingness of life. It could also be your experience with something tragic that brought growth to you—a loss, an unimaginable event, a turning point that threw open the doors and allowed heaven's light in.

These are all the first chapters of any spiritual seeker's life.

The Summer of 1977
My story begins when I was a child trying to make sense of a world that seemed to have lost its purpose and meaning. My mom died when I was eight, placing me in a role to help raise my five-year-old kid sister and my three-month-old baby sister. In 1973, child grief and assistance to understand my mother's transition were not present for me. I went through a series of babysitters and a nanny for close to a year until dad remarried.

Our family tried to form into some cohesive unit over the next few years by taking summer vacations, hoping to bring some semblance of being together as a happy experience. During one of the annual summer vacations, I found myself introduced to the feeling of prayer and the recognition of God in all things. It was as overwhelming and exhilarating as my first impression of the Atlantic Ocean, along what is known as the Delmarva Peninsula, an area of land that is a part of Virginia, Maryland, and Delaware.

Forever rolled out before my eleven-year-old eyes with the vastness of the Atlantic Ocean. The eastern horizon, curving in the periphery of my vision as I looked up and down the shoreline, was this dark line that demarcated the sky and the water. The beach was not this smooth, graceful, white sand flatness like the movies but an angular and sculpted form of compaction and human debris, from cigarette butts to lost sand-pail implements scattered up and down the pathway. Wherever I looked, I saw things that weren't beautiful in a romantic way but ordinary in how they were as they were.

In the hot August afternoon sun, I felt overpowered by the sound of the surf and the wildness of the other children and adults playing on the shore break and waves. The water boom hitting the packed sand was like a cannon in the parades that traveled down the main street in the town where I grew up. It felt like I was on a carnival ride, the ones that tilt and spin. It was so heady, and I was getting dizzy from the experience. I could feel myself easing into the sand beneath me to sit, absorbing this thing, to be with this Presence of being, something greater than anything I have ever known. Instead, I let my eyes go back to the horizon, and I felt myself being pulled into the unknown.

What is this thing, more powerful than anything I have ever felt, taking me to this state somewhere between imagination and reality? There was something out there, not the oyster and clam boats or barges that were barely visible from where I sat. Something that had been there since the beginning of time eternal called to me, letting me know how happy it was to see me. My senses were utterly pegged with excitement and anxiety as I could not see or grasp this energy, this force, whatever it was calling me

Chapter 1

and bringing me to it. I had to know it; I had to feel it; I had to run with it in the same zeal and mania that the children around me had splashing in the seafoam. I declared that by the end of the week, I would know what it was, this strange comforting feeling, this thing that felt so near.

The Child Who Finds Spirit

The following day, I slipped out of the rental house and went down the street to the end of the road, where the walkway started. It was barely six o'clock in the morning, and I was the only person there. I did not care about breakfast or what anyone else was doing at that hour. I made the deliberate choice to be out there by myself. It was the first time in my life that I felt I could be free to explore this feeling without anyone else's interference. There was no one to judge me, force me into dresses, or tell me to do other more lady-like things. I could be me! I was free like a breeze blowing the weather sock on the top of the house next to the dunes.

As I came upon the towers of a large wooden structure, I gasped. I could not believe what I saw in the early dawn. As I climbed the dunes, I saw the sun illuminate the water in the brightest green the instant it touched the horizon. It looked like it had dipped back in for a split second, turning the olive-colored waves into emeralds rolling to the sands.

As the waves crashed down, the seafoam danced like tiny white horses running up to the beach as far as they could reach before disappearing into the sandy wash. The sun moved up a little more, and it looked like someone cast diamonds everywhere on the sea. The ocean did not roar like it did the day before, but it seemed to coax me to its edge, to get me to touch the boundaries of its being along the wet sand.

I looked up and down the coast. I was alone. I knew better than to just jump into the surf, but the cool sandy wetness begged me to walk along its surface. I walked in the seafoam and let the water barely touch my feet. Along the edge of the beach, where the waves pulled back just enough to expose the hard pack of the sand, pebbles, and old seaweed clumps, I took in the textures with my toes and felt the salt spray on my face. It was heady and wild. My heart raced with delight.

Suddenly, I was running along the shoreline, flying as fast as I could with my arms opened wide like eagle wings. I splashed through the surf, jumping over the horseshoe crabs and barnacle piles that rolled up in the wash. I watched as the sky lit up in turquoise brilliance, clouds fading from apricot to white. It seemed I could fly right up to the clouds and dance with them in the sea breeze.

I was a child who would be a woman too soon, so different from her own family that it would be a defining moment later in my life. For now, I was happy and free, playing with God. I thought, "This must be what it feels like to be a part of God, to know this Presence, and to dance with the Almighty."

I slowed down and looked to see where I was in this delightful sprint and noticed I had lost sight of the towers that marked the pathway to return to my family. How far away was I? I could almost see the boardwalk. I ran nearly two miles up the shore.

The Epiphany

The distance I traveled would not compare to what Life had in store for me later in my life. Changes were coming, and I had no idea where it all would lead me to and take me from where I was on that beach. I could keep running, flying, splashing away but there was a sense that I needed to make a choice between running away and disappearing into this fantasy or accepting that there would be consequences for my little adventure away from the family. I decided to go back.

I wanted to take my time and enjoy myself with God. I felt loved and held by that something that had no form at all but loved me for who I was. It seemed It was just happy to be with me, and I was glad to be with whatever this thing was. I sensed I was coming to know that God wasn't what was depicted in the Sunday school I attended but was really more a part of me. As I walked back to the dunes and the old wooden towers, my feeling of God was love. God was all around me and walking with me back to where I started the morning. I was safe, and I was held in the Presence that had no name but was everything beautiful to me.

Within an hour, I found the towers and started making a sandcastle to mark my return. If my sisters or parents were looking for me, I would not be too hard to find. I got a broken pail from the dune and started pulling water out of the surf, bringing it up to the beach, and forming my eleven-year-old masterpiece.

The First Tithe and Prayer

A few days before we left for the family vacation, I got a ring at the dentist's office. I liked it because it was different from many other goodies in a bowl by the receptionist's desk. It was a little metal ring with a gold-colored diamond-shaped plate that had an image of a horse stamped on it. When I had the sandcastle the way I wanted it, I dug a hole between the two turrets. I took the ring off, set it in this place of honor, and buried it. It was my offering to God. I did not know if I would be able to slip out again like I did that morning, and I wanted to give God something that I appreciated as much as I did when I felt the love all around me. It was the only thing of value I had with me.

I would have tried to keep the ring because of what I saw as beautiful in my child's eyes, but I felt moved to let it go, to give away something I loved to something that loves me in the act of truth, respect, and faith. I knew the waves eventually would take the ring into the ocean to become part of all the treasures of the deep. I prayed the waves would come to take it and give it to God, that God could enjoy this ring, too.

My Life as Prayer

I knelt beside the sandcastle and looked around to see if anyone was watching me. I made my first prayer to God since my mom taught me to say prayers at bedtime when I was younger. I do not recall precisely what I said, but I remember some song that came into my head. To this day, I have no idea of the melody or harmony or what arrangement it could have been, but I knew in some way heaven was singing its love for me to me, through me, wrapping me up, to become a part of its foreverness of being. I felt so good, and I had not felt that good in so long. I never wanted to leave. I wanted to stay in that place, that peace of mind, forever and ever. I could feel the power of Love washing over me.

I looked up from my castle and saw the tide coming in. Before long, my castle and the ring would be a part of the ocean, given directly to God by the water itself. My prayer would be sealed on the shore, and my faith in God grew with the tide's reach as the sun climbed higher in the sky above me. The day's heat became noticeable as the sand and salt stung my toes when I finally pulled myself up from my kneeling prayer. I headed back to the rental, knowing God was always there for me no matter what.

Thinking of that Moment

Years later, the feelings of love and wonderment I experienced at the beach would come and go in my thoughts. In my best moments, in my worst moments, that rhythm and harmony that would synchronize to my heart would be near, always near. Even at certain points where I felt I should leave this plane of existence, its song would bring me back to this life. In those frustrating mornings with a partner, in the day-to-day affairs at my employment, when it seemed I could not do a single thing right that day, or when all was bliss for the week, there was this intonation holding me close.

Chapter 1

Many times, too many times, I could not hear the tempo of the waves on the sand because of the din in my head, the tiny voices that would gather en masse and dig into my ears to keep the music out. The voices of doubt, pain, fear, loathing, temptation, excess, all masochists for the taking in their schemes of belittling and wrenching me from my heart's desires.

There is nothing so painful as the fine art and skill of self-negation when all the world has for me is ready and available to me now, yet I choose not to partake in its offering. I could hear the hum of the melody continue though it never increased its volume, bass, or treble. It kept going and played, waiting for me to dance in its foreverness. I had choices, many that I followed to no worthy end. But the coherence was there, and it kept itself true to its inherent poetry. Over and over, I could hear the words, "I am with you," blending with the sounds of the sea. It waited patiently for me to turn around and take Its hand each time, and when I did, I was running along the sand with God in all my eleven-year-old glory.

When I pray, I begin with recognizing that God is in everything, everywhere, and is the very light, love, and joy I feel every minute of every day. The first part of prayer is recognizing God in all things, bringing forth the love I have for this life and how nature is the beauty I see and feel when I am in the Presence. I feel it in the pulse of my being, the blood and the breath moving through me, sustaining me in my physical form. I see the world and its beauty—the trees, the animals, the weather, the Earth's shape, and the oceans. I taste it in the wonderment of a snowflake or a meal lovingly given to me to enjoy. I smell it in the temple incense, the perfume of flowers, and the salty breeze by the bay. I hear it in the song of the birds, the music of the church, and the words that are still singing to my God song.

When the night comes, the Universe speaks, the stars shine, the comets fly, and the planets spin their orbits in a circle with the sun. When the day comes, the sun's warmth spreads like a blanket across the meadows and mountains, the deserts, and the grasslands, and all of creation rises with its light. My prayer is in this nature; it recognizes human nature as its beauty is affirmed in the morning, the allegory to all we know on this planet. It is all God, and it is all good.

Reflections

Listen for that voice, look for that sign, reach for that goal. We greet this new life with open arms and loving thoughts. We explore the land, the sky, and the waters around us and honor Spirit as we know Spirit to be. Our prayers, meditations, and hymns are heard and embraced in the beauty. We learn these things of our being, and we practice them.

We are practitioners for this reason—all of us. Some of us are licensed practitioners through the Centers for Spiritual Living, some are ministers, some are congregants, and some are simply the most spiritual beings ever to grace our lives. Let us take this first step, our recognition in this first part of affirmative prayer, this very first chapter in exploring the journey that takes us from where we are now to the most amazing heights of our existence. Recognition is essential in that it is this knowing of Life that is at the heart of the prayer, as it unfolds, the appreciation of Spirit in all things, places, and people.

This is the first chapter, the first step. We begin to move toward the unification of self and Self in our affirmative prayer process once we have mastered the recognition of Spirit in all things, persons, and beings. We know it, and we feel it. We move toward it. It comes into us, through us, and around us, washing over our feet like the waves along the sand, the wind on our faces, or the tears on our cheeks. We are all one under the same sun.

Chapter 1

Let forever come to us, pull us into It, and hold us always in the wonderment of our lives. Come dance with me as the sun rises over the water, across the sea, and brings the new day to us all. It is time, running along the water's edge with abandon, flying along with the clouds, holding onto the childlike sense of adventure in the unknown, yet replete with the knowingness of all there is, at this moment now.

A Prayer of Recognition

If this prayer speaks to you, please feel free to use it in your daily practice. If you want to change this prayer to assist you in writing your own prayer, I support you in your discovery and welcome your creativity.

The purpose of this prayer is to know and affirm that God is all there is.

> RECOGNITION: At this moment there is peace, love, and light abiding in the stars above and in the sunbeams that dance across the trees. The movement of the breeze moves with the flow of the water along the edge of the stream as it moves on to the river and the sea. The Essence is present and available, existing in every blade of grass and in each flower that grows in the garden. All of the wonders of our world are blessed and Spirit blesses us all.

> UNIFICATION: All is in the Oneness, the Divine Expression, the wholeness that God is and I am. Together as One, in One, through One, as a child of God, I am complete in Spirit and aligned in Oneness. As I know this for myself, all of the brilliance of nature surrounds me in light, love, and joy, the inherent happiness of All.

My Life as Prayer

REALIZATION: I declare that God is all there is in every step that I take, in every breath I breathe, in the very pulse of my being now. I affirm that Spirit is ever present in my life and in the lives of all sentient beings. The Essence moves and lives within all things as it moves and lives within me. All is God and all is well.

THANKSGIVING: With great gratitude and thanks, I experience the fullness and completeness of the blessings I receive and the reciprocation of love to all. To know and affirm the wonderment of Life is to be blessed. Thank you!

RELEASE: As I release my word into the Law, it is manifested infinitely and abundantly, fulfilled in the greatness of knowing that God is all there is. I let go and allow it to be. And so it is. Amen.

Chapter 2

Greeting Presence by Name

Unification: Spirit and I Are One

Unity as defined in the Science of Mind is the Oneness of God and man.... The word Unity, we might explain here, signifies the union of parts, a result of many drawn together into one perfect harmonious whole.... Oneness.... One Life of which we are a part; One Intelligence which we use; One Substance, which is brought into manifold manifestation.

—Ernest Holmes, *The Science of Mind,* pp. 640–641

Taking the Next Step

I came to a place in my life where I could no longer deny something so great and powerful; all I wanted to know was who or what this was. Some have said this is the proverbial night of the soul or the calling of one's shadow that summons this fabulous presence of understanding. Others have described it as that first light of day or the lightning bolt that shows up unexpectedly in a manner of beauty that is Divine.

I wish I could be so dramatic as to say this was an apocalyptic event for me or a dreamy fantasy come true in real time. It actually felt more like when a car runs out of gas and rolls to a stop in the middle of nowhere. No hobgoblins or demons sprang out from the roadside. No magical mechanical angels flew in from the nearest garage to revive the vehicle. Instead, everything slowed until there was not anything left to keep my thoughts distracted and my head fully inserted someplace else.

The 1980s and the Challenges that Came Forward

Becoming a military police officer was not what I wanted to do, but I did it as my life was going nowhere. Bombing out of preliminary medical studies while in college because the subjects I took were way out of my league and not what I wanted to do, I was upset that there was no way my family was going to let me change to an English major. It seemed I did not have too many options, and I needed to make some serious decisions.

In 1984, unemployment hovered at around 17 percent in some areas of the United States. I was suddenly faced with making

My Life as Prayer

beds at the local hotels and living temporarily under my parents' roof. My only way out of there and the small-town mindset was to go into the military and somehow find my way to what I wanted to do in life. Unfortunately, the only military recruiter available when I went to sign up was an Army sergeant looking to make his quota before the month was out. My options were to go into avionics and work on helicopters, be a coordination clerk in the Quartermaster Corps, or become a military police officer. My choices for my first duty stations were South Korea, Germany, Panama, or Hawaii. I took Hawaii without a second thought.

I wound up stationed in what I learned was the most beautiful place in the world and viewed as the laziest duty a military police officer could pull. For a brief time during my stint in Hawaii, I was assigned to a "resort" area along the leeward side of the island. It was nothing more than three-quarters of a mile filled with rock and sand for designated military use as recreation only. A sandy swath of a lagoon—built up with jetties, weekend military cabin rentals, a package store and bar, and a cast of characters from the surrounding area who enjoyed overrunning the grounds at will—it was an MP paradise. People wound up here either because the commander decided you needed a break from the intensity of your duties, or you were running close to disciplinary proceedings for something no one wanted to deal with, and this was the next best place for you. For me, it was a little of both.

I had hit a point where nothing seemed to make sense. I was a mess from partying, long shift work, and becoming depressed with everything I was doing. I either pulled myself together or I had orders to leave the islands. As I watched MTV in the bar one afternoon, I felt like this was as good as things would get. Here I was in MP limbo, and now I had to wait and see if I would be going back to my primary duty station or find myself re-assigned

Chapter 2

to something else. I was tired of pacing the lanai and chasing the kids out of the package store.

My brain was going numb with the correspondence courses I needed to do for my promotion to Specialist E-4, and there was no challenge in the studies. In fact, I could create patterns of Christmas trees, race cars, and zig-zag dots all over the test card and still wind up with an 80 percent passing score. I took an introductory police sciences class from the University of Hawaii, but that did not interest me—just another peg toward my military police advancement and enhancement.

Did I want to spend the rest of my life in the military?

Self-Discovery at a Thrift Store
The next day I went over to a thrift store in town one of my friends recommended for cheap books. If I did not start working on something that got my brain in gear and moving, something I believed was intelligent and thought-provoking, I would be a lifer. Within twenty years, I would be institutionalized entirely by a system I wanted nothing to do with.

I wandered over to a bookcase with everything from children's books to empty photo albums. There was no alphabetical sense to it. I had to look along each shelf to find anything that seemed to say it was better than scratch and sniff.

The lady running the place saw I was lost in my endeavor and asked what I wanted. I told her I wanted something to get me to think about my life differently. She pointed to three books on the shelf and told me this was all she had in philosophy. Philosophy? I had no idea that philosophy was what I needed, but I grabbed Jean-Paul Sartre's *Existentialism*, handed her a dollar, and took it back to the barracks.

It took me three weeks to read it, and by the time I finished, not only was I questioning why I existed and the purpose of my existence, but I also wondered whether I would look cool in a black beret with a cigarette and a tiny cup of espresso in a French café. This was not what I needed, and I gave it back to the thrift shop to resell to someone who could appreciate the book.

The lady at the thrift store asked me to give philosophy another try and read another book with Albert Camus's treatise on the absurd. Once I succeeded in understanding Camus, philosophy did not feel like such a wrong starting place. Before long, I read several classics, from Lewis Carol to C.S. Lewis, Twain to Tennyson, and I dabbled with poetry and biographies on Picasso, O'Keeffe, Kahlo, and other artists and writers. I truly enjoyed the thrift store because I got to read all the Ernest Hemingway novels, and the owner introduced me to the writings of Suzuki, Dogen, and other Zen Buddhist scholars.

Expanding my reading list started me writing and journaling beyond my regular police reports, sometimes sitting up after shift to contemplate Basho. I began to pull away from the bizarre Christian structure I knew as a child, a strange compilation of Catholic thought and Southern Evangelical Baptist discipline. All the while, I had no idea I had just taken a step to know God for myself, the Almighty as I understood Spirit to be.

The Night Shift

There are moments I cannot explain but that just happened at times. Some of the MPs had told me that being left in limbo at the resort was a place of unusual things and happenings, but I thought that meant being unlucky or running into some weird spooky stuff. When the station sergeant moved me to the night shift for a few weeks, I was almost thrilled to do something other than chasing kids away from the beer trucks and making sure that higher-ranking officers were not embarrassing themselves with excessive alcoholic beverage consumption.

My only jobs and duties for the night shift were to ensure no one was trespassing and that all loud parties were complete by

Chapter 2

midnight. I would shake the closed package store and bar doors to ensure everything was secured and all the alarms were set. I would do walk-arounds between the cabins and double checks along the lanai to avoid falling asleep in the cove. It really wasn't too bad, and I could still go surf later in the day if I wanted to.

On an auspicious evening, after a couple of weeks on the night shift, I found out something not discussed in Sunday school was closer to me than the helmet on my head. It had nothing to do with French ponderings on life or color television sets. It had everything to do with recognizing another human being's soul.

Prelude to a Chance Encounter

Beach people, as the homeless folks were often referred to by both military personnel and civilians, would try to hide out along the jetties when the marina on the other side of the Army beach shut down for a few hours. They would wait until the fishing boats came in around three or four in the morning and try to find a boat that needed someone to clean the catch. Often, they were avoiding being chased off by the local police during a sweep of the docks by the marina security officers. It wasn't unusual to find one or two folks trying to come up onto the Army beach, passing themselves off as fishing for eels in the crevices of the jetties or as guests of a guest at one of the cabins.

We knew about a homeless Vietnam veteran who traveled with a particular group of beach people and was known to live in the area.. His face was on the station wall, an AWOL from 1974, yet we could never catch him. He had walked off the personnel transport airplane at one of the Air Force bases and was not seen again. We were warned that if we found him, we were not to make contact and should get backup support right away. We were never told why he was so threatening; these were orders we had to follow. Legend had it he beat up a military police officer in the cove, but no one knew when that happened, and it seemed few folks wanted to speak to that incident.

One evening, I suddenly had a strange feeling come over me, and I realized I was not alone in the cove. I was checking the area to make sure no one was sleeping on the picnic tables or camping in the lean-to. I used my nightstick to move the coconut tree leaves and debris from the high tide that washed in along the jetties. I pulled down palm fronds from the back of the chain-link fence, just in case someone was under there, too. The moon was full and bright that evening. It was almost as light as daytime, if it were not for the heavy dark shadows and pinkish tint of the lights of the barracks, highlighting the lean-to in the cove. It was weird, surreal, and otherworldly in a place people called paradise. I could not see who it was, but I could feel their presence. Dark, heavy, intent on something nefarious, someone watching me for no good reason at all.

The closest MP to me was on the other side of the beach patrolling the cabins. I keyed my mic and called for backup, but the radio did not work. An eerie silence and the weirdness of the moonlight gave me chills, and I felt spooked. There was no wind, no movement in the broken clouds above me, and the stars were barely visible in the bright moonlight. I walked back to the barracks to get another radio, moving quickly as my fright started to get the best of me.

The Eyes of a Lost Soul

Out of the corner of my eye, I saw him. It was the AWOL soldier from 1974, the man I had seen countless times on the station wall. He came around the jetty and ran at me, looking like some demon released from the sea. He moved fast, keeping that speed up until I pulled my nightstick out to swing at him. He slowed down and gathered the rain poncho he was wearing to one side and the other to show he had no weapon.

Chapter 2

The stench coming from him was horrible, and to this day, I have never experienced a smell so bad that I almost threw up. His clothing was soiled, and I did not want to identify what was on his T-shirt and pants. The man was not well, breathing hard as he stopped short in front of me, his whole demeanor fraught with anger. His face was so pale it appeared as white as a piece of paper. He appeared young, but he had to be close to his forties. The gaunt frame of his body showed he had not eaten well for a very long time.

It was his eyes that startled me more than him running at me and scaring me to death. They were lifeless dark spheres, hollows in a face that had to have known something so evil as to take the light out of the windows to his soul. There was nothing in his eyes, just darkness and this bottomless pain from pure hell. Where is this man's joy? Was it ever there? I felt I was staring into the bleakness of a bottomless pit filled with memories of death and despondency.

We stood about seven feet apart. My training taught me that most gun and knife fights were often deadly at this distance, and I wasn't convinced he did not have something hiding under the poncho. Everything stopped at that moment—my heartbeat, breath, and hearing. My eyes were locked on this guy, and only one thing came to mind: Don't die at this man's hands.

He seemed stunned and perplexed that I was there. A female MP was challenging him, and he had no idea what to do. He took a step, tears started to well up in the veteran's eyes, and a slight smile broke to reveal his missing teeth. His poncho had fallen over his arms, and I could not tell if he was ready to pull out a knife or a firearm. The poncho's hood slipped to reveal a messy, oily pile of curls on top of his head, and the moonlight made this greasy mess glimmer with a silvery light.

I no longer saw a vile and putrid human being in front of me; I saw a deeply hurt man who could not tell me his pain. He was angelic, and he was fearsome. His humanity ripped my heart out, and I felt a commonality with him. The tears he cried left tracks on his cheeks, and he looked at me like a little boy needing a friend to guide him home. Was he that dangerous? For God's sake, he's a hurting unit and I am about add to his woes by simply showing up, enforcing more injury into his life.

I could not imagine what he may have been through, and thoughts raced through me, wondering if I would wind up like him. The darkness of his eyes still bothered me and would not let me release their agonizing ache to see again. Is this my existence, too? Would I be able to express myself humanely? Would someone also see my eyes as hazel and alive to the world? Am I lost in the horror of another place and time, left to wander along some forsaken part of an island that is heaven to those with plenty and hell to those who have nothing? He and I were recognizable to one another for a brief second, a oneness that transcended into a connection from this lostness we both had within us.

The Escape

Slowly his hands began to come out from under the dirty rain poncho. He may have been attempting a gesture of surrender, but I wasn't waiting to find out if he was about to bring out something else from underneath the poncho. My hand instinctively swung my nightstick up to knock his arms down and push him away from me. Without a radio to call for help, I was facing my own destiny, and I had to make this decision for my own safety. If he lunged for the revolver on my hip, this story as I am telling it now would never be written.

Stunned that I was about to hit him, he pulled his hood up and looked right at me, and for the first time, I could see his eyes were brown, and there was a brief flicker of life. He started to shake as if he were having a seizure. He mumbled incoherently, then followed it with the most banshee-like scream I ever heard, piercing my ears in a way I have never forgotten. He violently shook his head to say no, to keep me from apprehending him. I was in complete shock. Weren't he and I the same, in some way, ruined by what we were told to believe, and now we see that the truth is we are who we are, on different levels of reality, at this very moment?

I had no idea what he had planned for me in the next moment, and he did not know if I would injure him in the next instant that followed. The connection was gone another second later, and now there was only the length of my nightstick separating him from me.

Another MP on patrol saw him round the corner of the jetty and ran down to assist me as I braced for a possible takedown. The veteran stood there, waiting for the other MP to get within a few feet of me, then lunged past us.

As hard and as fast as I ran after the veteran, he was gone into the shadows in the blink of an eye. I turned, and he was gone, vanished somewhere between the barracks and the gate shack at the end of the drive. Even with the other military police officer and I running between the buildings, dashing through the barracks and guest cabins to catch him, he got away without indicating he had ever been there. The MP on gate duty saw nobody pass her or head toward town. No one else saw him; it was as if we were the only witnesses to a ghost.

Reflections

Denying service to someone looking for help was an atrocity to me. Yet, in a moment for which I was trained to react, I almost injured someone who needed me to see who he was and be one with the expression he was trying to demonstrate. I allowed him to disappear without a connection to his need. This would bother me for years until I, too, reached out for help.

My Life as Prayer

Intellectually, I was lost in college before I joined the service. In my brief year at school, what little I gained somehow provided a sense of need to feed my curious mind with things I believed were important. I believed it was necessary to be known and to be recognized by others in some way that society would approve of, that my family would approve of, that the military would approve of. I had to put aside the person I knew myself to be for approval and acceptance, a far cry from the ballsy expectations I had to fulfill as a military police officer in the Army.

There is no separation from Spirit. The AWOL soldier and I were one, however brief that connection was, as I saw him as a human being, and he saw me for who I was, too. That momentary bond brought life to him and reciprocated the wholeness I had lost. We were healed as his truth and my truth were made known without a single word spoken. All is One, all is God.

These incomplete and incomprehensible moments brought me to unify with God and know Presence by name as I knew the name to be. It is one of the most challenging things to do and admit that Spirit is and I am; we are one. It is the easiest thing to do when we recognize that Spirit is in all things, people, and places. When we greet Presence by name, we see the truth of our connection and divinity at that moment, and we are synonymous with It. There are no disconnections; there are always connections. There are no disappointments; there are always appointments with the Divine. We are all One, and what we feel, know, experience, and complete ourselves with, Spirit meets within us.

Unification became as disjointed as I was trying to find myself in intellectual pursuits and capturing people who escaped me. To know Spirit is to connect with Spirit, as Spirit, in Spirit. Despite having a lack of tangible connection, there were times I did have a spiritual connection. Feeling the fright of the AWOL and my heartbreak that the help he needed he was too scared to receive, I was pained to know the veteran resorted to moving through town undercover, with an old Army-issued poncho as his only shelter.

When knowledge comes through, those hurts and heartbreaks become passages that allow Spirit to come through us. In other practices that enable unification, this becomes central to the path I walk with Spirit as one. God is, and I am, and I recognize the good in others and wonder about the wisdom given through story and learning. Truth is inseparable from oneness, and this is unification at its core.

A Prayer of Unification

If this prayer speaks to you, please feel free to use it in your daily practice. If you want to change this prayer to assist you in writing your own prayer, I support you in your discovery and welcome your creativity.

The purpose of this prayer is to affirm that God is and I am.

RECOGNITION: The ocean's balance is held in the hands of the Earth and the moon through the rise and the fall of the tides, in perfect precision, with the movement of the waves on the water's surface. In the perfection of the moment, the tide rises, and in the perfection of time that follows, the tide recedes. The Essence moves with the tides, flowing easily and effortlessly in and out of our lives, blessing the time and space in loving grace. This is Spirit in motion, and it touches the shores of my being.

UNIFICATION: Spirit and I are One, whole, unified, oneness defined and perfected in light, love, and joy. As a child of God, I find the completeness and brilliance of this Oneness to be effervescent, wrapped in the Spirit that is always present. I know this for myself as I know this for everyone, for we are all children of God. We are all One.

My Life as Prayer

REALIZATION: I declare that Oneness fulfills every sentient being, every person, and all seekers of this spiritual path we call life. We are one family on this planet Earth, we are Divine and we are the embodiment of Light, Love, and Joy, uninhibited and unchained by any extremes presented in our experience. We are Wholeness personified, we are all children of God, the brilliance that shines for all to see and know the Oneness of our existence.

THANKSGIVING: It is with great gratitude that I see and know the beauty all around me that is the wonder of the appreciation for Life. I am thankful to be present in this time and space, witness to the Unity and the perfection of All. Thank you.

RELEASE: As I release my word into the Law, the unity expressed in this prayer is fulfilled and manifested infinitely now. Blessing upon blessing is abundant and known to All, and so it is. Amen.

RELEASE: As I release my word into the Law, the realization of the Truth of Life in its beauty and wholeness manifests abundantly and infinitely. It is fulfilled and complete, and so it is. Amen.

Chapter 3

Walking a Path Unknown

Realization: I Accept and Become the Good in My Life

The word realization, at any time, means an impression of reality on the mind; a clear apprehension; an acceptance of the mind that a thought or condition is actual.... When we speak of "a perfect realization", we are referring to a realization of our Oneness with Good.

—Ernest Holmes, *The Science of Mind*, pg. 625

Finding the Spiritual Truth
"I have been there." "We have all been there." Every time I heard that phrase, that we've been there or here or wherever, I could feel the annoyance building, including my not-so-subtle tendency to want to throw something because that phrase just drove me nuts. The phrase "ad nauseum" made me just as nauseous. And I practically wanted to burn every self-help book I found.

I felt intense anger in my thirties as I struggled to get over myself and all the commotion I was allowing to control my life, from stupid people stunts to random acts of idiocy. I was hellbent on destroying myself physically and mentally, stuck in a dead-end assembly job on the Front Range and playing cowgirl on an amateur rodeo circuit. I was broke financially, spiritually, and who knows where else I was broken. I chased all kinds of stuff just like I tracked the calves to rope. I chased dreams right to the bottom of every emotional pit of despair. All I did was chase. What was I chasing? If I had "been there," where was everybody else? They probably were burning their self-help books, too.

Besides my book-burning fantasies, I would oblige my time and energy for a few bucks by taking care of other people's ranch needs if they had to leave town. I had agreed to take care of a horse named Dolly when my friend had to leave town for a family matter. It seemed I was always taking care of somebody's horse, one way or the other.

My Life as Prayer

Meeting Dolly

I drove out to the eastern plains to my friend's place. It was near a county road in what would be considered the middle of nowhere, just short of who knows where, closer to Kansas, if anywhere. I found the horse had wandered to the far end of the pasture and was up to her knees in mud. I walked out and called for Dolly, and she lumbered and plodded her way out of the puddles. Just as I was thinking that wiping all that mud would take a good long while, she let me know she had another task for me. The horse looked right at me, and I knew something was up because if that old nag could smile, she certainly would. Dolly eased herself down and rolled in the mud, not once but twice, to make sure she got both sides of herself soaked. Instantly, I had an all-night grooming session with Dolly, and she was waiting for me to get started on it and finish by sundown. Thankfully, I had the next day off from my commute into town to work on those assembly lines.

I walked back to the shed and got a bucket of grain to coax her out of the puddles. Dolly was not budging, and the flies were ferocious in the late afternoon heat. I went back to the shed for a fly mask, and sure as anything, Dolly had hiked up to the grain bucket and emptied it, turned, and proceeded back into the mud. There was no changing that old mare, and I could see that the grooming would take a couple of hours; convincing her to come up to the shelter would take some heft. I said I would do this, and clearly, the hundred dollars I was getting to keep an eye on Dolly for the weekend was going to be earned the hard way.

I walked out into the mud with her. It did not matter that I had irrigation boots on; I went right down to my mid-thigh on the first step. I was in the thick of the muck in the middle of nowhere and wondered how I would move close enough to get the fly mask, halter, and lead rope on without swimming out to her.

Dolly must have had pity on me or thought it was interesting to see an immobilized human stranded in the mire. She wandered over to me and gave me a shove with her head, and in I went, face first. I pulled myself up quickly, spitting out the mire and wiping my face off the best I could. I was head to toe in the slop, and Dolly seemed to admire how it coated every inch of me. I had no spare clothes. I wondered if anyone out there would notice I drove back home naked.

Dolly's shove was hard enough to push me to where I found some footing, and I could stand where the mud was not so deep. I agreed with the horse; the murky earth certainly kept the flies off me. Wiping my eyes, I saw the fly mask and the halter sunk into the puddles, but the rope was still manageable with little pasture stuff stuck to it. Dolly walked up onto the drier part of the field and waited for me to take her to the shelter. I pulled the mask and the halter out of the mud and tossed them onto the fence to dry out. I sloshed up to Dolly and put the lead rope around her neck. I was glad that part of the effort was complete.

I was happy to walk alongside Dolly to the shelter, mud spilling out of my boots and clods bouncing off her hooves.

The Clean Up

I got another bucket with some senior feed for her and set it down while I got the hose and hooked it up to the barn spigot. I looked at the garden thermometer. It said it was eighty-seven degrees as of four o'clock, and I felt it even with the slime all over me. I got another halter on the horse and then tied her to the post. As I turned on the water, making sure I pointed the hose away from her until I got the pressure right, I felt how icy the well water was coming through it. We both just got out of a steamy pasture pond, and now I was about to wash her down with ice water. Maybe I can chip the mud off of her tomorrow?

My Life as Prayer

She saw what I was doing and got still. I was not sure if this was a good idea, to bathe the horse by myself, but it needed to be done, and the smell of pond scum and road apples was starting to get nasty as the mud began to dry on me. I started slowly with her front hooves, practically making as much mud as from where we walked out just a few minutes ago. She did not budge, and she lowered her head softly, almost as if it felt relieving to her. I carefully did the back hooves and, with super slow-motion movements, brought the hose to her haunches, letting the water gently pull the grime off her skin and coat.

Dolly let me soak her back, hold her tail and drench it, and even allowed me to spray her neck down carefully. I got her chest, her tummy, and the insides of her legs. I stepped back and admired the dapple-grey spots on her hide, showing her Appaloosa and quarter-horse breeds. She was such a gorgeous animal, solid and sturdy at twenty-seven years young. She had the "appie blanket" across her rump—the white and black spots against her roan coat of steel grey and chestnut. I soaped her and got her good and foamy, talking to her about my appreciation for her quietness. I hosed her down again, the same way, then dried her off.

I was getting cleaned up in the process, but I still seriously needed a shower. I saw the fly bites near her ears and on her flank. I walked to the barn and got some ointment to put on the oozy sores and bumps. She gave me a soft whiny and lowered her head to let me put the balm on the fly bites. I set the ointment can down and started to check her legs and hooves for any more issues. After putting the lotion on, I got a pick, lifted her hooves, and cleaned them. The last thing to do was to take some time combing out her tail and mane. She liked that quite a lot. I let her rest there and got a couple of flakes of sweetgrass for her trough, mucked out her stall, and put down fresh pine shavings. I sprayed her with fly spray and rubbed it in with a soft cloth.

Chapter 3

Walking over to her stall, I checked the fly strips in her shelter to see if they needed to be removed or new ones put up. The evening sun was perfect, lighting everything in an orange hue like a Hallmark movie. There was perfection at that moment; it felt as though the truth of her being a horse and my reality of being a human were being framed in this evening God light.

I led her back to the stall and put her in. Every step seemed to be the right step. Her steps were the rhythm of the day slipping by, and my steps were cautious with her. I let her into the stall and took the lead rope off her. She went up to her manger as I closed the stall door to walk away. All of a sudden, I heard a loud thud. My heart skipped a beat as I ran back to her. There she was, rolling in the dust and horse poop in the paddock outside of her stall, an open area just off to the side of the manger, completely content. She swished her tail, and rolled up onto her feet, happily farting back to her trough to continue eating. Good golly, Dolly!

Putting Things Away
I found a denim jacket in the barn and a pair of overalls while I picked up the gear from cleaning Dolly. I got a pair of boots out of the trunk of my car, and I knew those would wind up rubbing my bare feet raw, but the drive back to my home was only about an hour; I could kick the boots off when I got back in the car. My clothes were now beyond washable recovery, so I grabbed the hose and went between the barn and the tractor to clean up and change. I sprayed what I could off me. I could not tell if the cold water did any good with the smell on me, but it certainly woke me up.

I looked over at Dolly, who had stopped in mid-chew to watch the human try to handle bathing in cold water. She grunted and turned away, completely unimpressed. I took the clothes over to the dumpster and tossed them in, finding my friend had clothes just as bad in there from mud bathing, too. One of Dolly's favorite games, as it appeared to me, is to muddy up the humans and have them put on a shower show for her.

I walked over to brush her off before leaving. The sun was down now, but there was enough twilight I could still see where I could get some of the dirt off Dolly before calling it a night. She came out and leaned against the corral fence so I could climb it and get to the heavier stuff on her back. I was revealing the truth without ever knowing that grooming a horse would help me find my way to my own happiness.

Dolly and the Realization

It struck me as I was getting the last bit of grooming done how my life had gotten to be the way it was. I was crazy happy on the beach as a child, and I went through some abrupt turns in the Army. I allowed so much to distract me and destroy the good I knew myself to be. What Dolly taught me that evening was precisely what the lady in the thrift store on the islands was trying to do, helping me embrace the Buddhist teachings she grew up with, sharing with me to know what happiness was in life.

Dolly standing in the mud to escape the flies demonstrated suffering and how she ended that suffering. When she quietly rested and allowed me to bathe and clean her up, she was meditating on that moment in the now. When she flopped down in her stall and rolled, she showed me what life teaches in alleviating suffering. Dolly is a horse; she will do horsey things; she lives her day entirely in the mud if she chooses. I am a human, I will do human things, and I live my life like a toxic spill by my choosing.

Realizing I needed more than horse sense to get out of my mud-hole, Dolly showed what happiness is to me. Dolly is accepted as a horse; she does not need anyone to tell her she is anything but a horse. I am accepted as a human being, not a faux rodeo star or a one-time G.I. Jane. A horse has its spirit, and it never breaks. No matter how tame people think horses are, they are not the animations watched on Saturday morning children's shows. Dolly knows Spirit is always there.

When was the last time, since that morning on that East Coast beach, I stopped and said, "I love you, God"? While I was not dealing with flies like Dolly, I let the atrocities I experienced nip and bite at me, then I allowed myself to fall into the well of lost hopes and desires. Dolly is a Zen master, and I am her student.

Dolly awakened me to my truth. Could I move from this to that which I am? And what am I now? Did all this trouble, iniquity, and drive to die before forty make up for what I had to take responsibility for in this? How many face plants in the muck and slime did I need before I realized I was letting things put me there?

The very ends of the Earth were not enough for me to challenge one of many obstacles to my greatness. It took a horse and a field full of mud to allow me to realize I was worthy of life.

What was going on was something else I did not see yet in the swill. The joy I once knew as a child was still there. My grit and courage showed me the ability to walk on a path unknown and stay with it. The fact that I kept to my dreams of art and writing and being wise to the world around me was the very essence of life. Childlike and brutal, muddied and roughed up, I became my truth.

Reflections

Now is that time—from recognizing Spirit in all things to knowing that all things, including myself, are One. In that, Oneness comes forward to realize the spiritual truths of ourselves and others. We know this and declare it for ourselves and others. The truth is that I am whole and perfect just as I am, in every way.

Although I know this, I declare it as much as I feel and experience All in my bones, All in myself, All in the world I live and exist in. I am beautiful in the eyes of Spirit as One, and in this Oneness, I am the essence expressed as this unique wonderment. I declare and claim this for myself as much I do for others; may they see, touch, and hold this light, love, and joy within themselves with the very brilliance of the Light within them.

In *Living the Science of Mind,* Ernest Holmes talks about how important it is that we connect ourselves with Spirit. We realize the truth of who we are in the moment now and declare it, claim it, and know it beyond the shadow of a doubt. When we see this fantastic beauty, we embrace that full-on connection to something more significant than ourselves. We are that, not "this." In *Living the Science of Mind,* Holmes talks about a person's happiness with themselves: "Did you ever notice the contagion of a happy person, one who has an enthusiastic joy in living? His spirit permeates those around him, and the contagion of his personality influences his environment to such an extent that it finally changes it."

A Prayer of Realization

If this prayer speaks to you, please feel free to use it in your daily practice. If you want to change this prayer to assist you in writing your own prayer, I support you in your discovery and welcome your creativity.

The purpose of this prayer is to realize the wholeness and beauty of Life

> RECOGNITION: In the evening light, the beauty and perfection of all life, the Essence is present in the twilight, moving into the starlight on the horizon. The moment of transition between the day and the night progresses with ease and all of Life prepares to gaze upon the Universe opening in the sky above. A thousand diamonds of light brighten the way to the Cosmos, bringing forward the Divine in all.

Chapter 3

UNIFICATION: Coming together now, Spirit and I are One, as One, in One, and through One. In this Oneness, all is well, unified in the Perfection that is, the knowingness that I am a child of God. As I know this for myself, I know this and recognize that the Presence in all life is realized fully, lovingly, and joyously expressed in this Oneness.

REALIZATION: This expression is truth, the deep knowingness of Life in each and every one of us, the light in the sky, and the blessings of the Earth beneath our feet. I declare that Life is whole, wonderful, and beautiful in infinite ways, as expressed in this moment now. The greatness of All is present, now and always.

THANKSGIVING: It is with great gratitude that I am blessed to experience the beauty and wholeness of Life. A thousand thank you's fill my heart, and I reciprocate this love to All and to everyone, feeling this abundance moving through me. It is precious, and I indulge in the good as it is given.

RELEASE: As I release my word into the Law, the realization of the Truth of Life in its beauty and wholeness manifests abundantly and infinitely. It is fulfilled and complete, and so it is. Amen.

Chapter 4
Gifts, Blessings, and Other Miscellanea

Thanksgiving: Thank You

When we speak the words of thanksgiving to the God within, knowing "before they ask I will answer," there is something in this attitude of thanksgiving that carries us beyond the field of doubt, into one of perfect faith and acceptance.

—Ernest Holmes, *The Science of Mind,* pg. 637

Appreciation of Life's Offerings
I was driving home from my eighth job in seven years. My relationship had been on the rocks for more than six of those eight years, and I was in deep denial. I had started out becoming more financially secure and having better opportunities for advancement, a home, a decent vehicle, and all the accruements of wealth. Now I was once again looking for work at a staffing agency to keep my finances and relationship stable. What had appeared as a good relationship for many years turned out to be the most ridiculous ruse. It was all a façade. If I were grateful for this union for a minute, I lost it in a second.

Here I was, playing chauffeur to someone who benefited from all my efforts for success. This would include the disambiguation of my old military and cowgirl ways, parts of me that did not adapt well to some aspects of society but still held a place in my personality. Without those periods in my life, I may not have been able to get as far as I did.

I could not find anything that appeared to be acceptable to my partner's schedule and ideal life. I often spent ten to fourteen hours a day at work to create some form of financial stability. I continually moved from place to place to find that elusive perfect life balance. The new circumstances always seemed to wind up being too good to be true, I found myself grossly underpaid, and I was allowing it all to be so. Once again, I was driving home to another miserable evening with no time for myself and another

My Life as Prayer

round of having to deal with more woe-is-me sob stories from my other half.

I could not get over the whole gamut of disappointments in my life since the start of our relationship, from losing my fantastic pay years ago to now earning a living well below what I used to make through a succession of fly-by-night manufacturing companies. The bills piled up, and the credit ran dry.

Finding Grace

Though I did not want to interview for another aerospace job, knowing the stress and intensity of the minutia I would deal with in quality assurance, the staffing company insisted, and I felt this was the only way to make any money. It was the best outcome I could see for keeping my head above water, if only the tip of my nose, to get out of this financial debacle. I would have to begin again on the low end of the pay scale, and starting pay was four dollars an hour better than what I was making at the time. I would be less than ten minutes from home, and I would feel better about myself as an inspector in this type of engineering world.

Working on manufacturing lines and in the construction yards in my late forties and early fifties had become hard on my body, though some of the work no doubt kept me physically more robust than most women my age. I had someone I was supporting, and since things had not improved in years, I needed to take this job.

My partner and I spent several years volunteering at various nonprofit organizations between my periods of unemployment and underpaid endeavors. It was a way to distract me and to find something to point a path toward a source of income that would inspire my partner to move forward in life.

As it turned out, all of it was doing more for me than it was for anything else. I began building on things that made me more compassionate and in tune with the world around me. I learned about people with autism and cerebral palsy as they found ways to adapt to riding a horse and to engaging with the world around them. I learned new ways of caring for livestock, cats, and dogs by becoming an animal reiki practitioner.

I also knew that the place I took myself away from years ago was where I needed to be. I needed to go back to my church.

Coming Home, Again

I was introduced to the teachings of Ernest Holmes by friends who dropped me off at Mile Hi Church in Lakewood, Colorado, on a Sunday in May 2002. They felt this would help me out by doing something other than getting into trouble with some of the other groups I ran around with at the time. They wanted me to do this on my own at least once to see what the teaching was all about. After my first visit, I was thrilled to know there was this place where everyone was accepted and where all the religions of the world had a voice in spiritual discovery. When the practitioners came out, wearing their purple stoles and beaming with happiness, I wanted to be one of those folks right away.

After a time, my friends did not want to go back. They said they brought me there to give me something to do and help me find other people to hang out around. They believed I wasn't smart enough to be a practitioner, and it was a foolish thing for me to do, that I would need years of education in psychology, theology, or sociology. Some friends!

As my life changed and other things began to happen outside of the church, I left for twelve years to continue improving myself and working myself to the bone spiritually and financially. In 2016, I returned to Mile Hi Church and reignited my interest in the study of Religious Science. I began to heal and see that when I said I wanted to become a practitioner, I was ready. Now was that time. My relationship was over, stumbling through something neither one of us was equipped to handle. The relationship I needed was with God; the life satisfaction I wanted was here.

Opening to a New Path

It had been lost on me for far too long. I was hearing, but I was not listening. I was sensing, but I was not feeling. I was empty, but I was not filling myself with the love, light, and joy that would be sufficient for my journey. A practitioner seemed to me to be an immensely prayerful person who had some pathway to God that I hadn't allowed myself to venture into. Yet, I wanted that ability to pray so profoundly and earnestly in knowing all was well and all was God.

A practitioner knows the spiritual truth of the client they work with. As a channel of this truth, a practitioner brings forward the good in others through the power of affirmative prayer. Was I brave enough to challenge myself to be a channel to bring forward the good in others, too?

Where do I start? How do I get there? What do I need to do? Who do I talk to or see or learn from about these things? Why am I even here thinking about being a practitioner nearly fifteen years later? I should be spending time making up for all my financial losses and getting my act together. But I had changed. The world had changed. My relationship had changed.

I personally freaking cannot stand change, but that fear of change in me also changed. I took a job because I believed I had nowhere else to validate myself and have money. I cared for other people's responsibilities and left behind my own needs. I went somewhere to find out who I am and became a pawn in someone else's chess game.

I lost my childhood to find my way back to being a child of God.

There was a girl who played on a beach and found her happiness. There was a soldier who served halfway around the world and understood something of someone's truth. There was a cowgirl who did whatever she could to care for this world and received it in the love of an animal, the earth, and the day's fading light. There was a woman, hardened by her egotistic sense of direction, physically injured, mentally exhausted, and spiritually oblivious, a woman who dared to walk before everyone and roar, "I am a practitioner!" Yes, I said that.

I was blessed with a difficult childhood that led me to find something extraordinary on an unkempt beach. It showed me that despite the trash and garbage washed ashore, there was a purity to be found on those sands. I felt safe enough to allow something of value to be shared with something even more significant than I could describe. I explored my creativity and let my imagination create a sandcastle that would be my dream fortress. We see sandcastles as fragile and dissolving into nothingness beneath an ocean wave, but where would we start to build those dreams without a sandcastle?

Spirit has been with me always; things will always travel with us if we choose. In his book *Creative Ideas*, Ernest Holmes states, "If God is our creator and refuge, why is it that we refuse to avail ourselves of this divine security? It appears we cannot experience the action of God in our lives until we first turn to God until we embody those things which are of the nature of God."

Reflections

I became something outside of myself, outside my creative nature, absorbing the fear of never expressing myself. Some folks might run off to join the circus; I ran off and joined the military police. This is so commonplace for people to do. Not going off into the Army, mind you, but separating from the Good that wants to come through us all, to be One. In spiritual terms, there is so much more to love in one another. Together as One, in One, and through One, we can all enjoy our lives in much more fulfilling ways. When I started to see that the only person I could go to who might make sense of human things was me, I also began that journey of wonder to know what I could go to and know God.

There are practices in all thoughts, religions, philosophies, and spiritual connections to the Divine but none more powerful and expansive as the unity of God. Referring to *Creative Ideas*, we see Holmes continues, "We cannot experience love while we hate. Neither can we enjoy the peace while we remain confused." What a blessing to know that God speaks in me, around me, and through me, in the thoughts and experiences I received at moments of great pain and misunderstanding.

To state that life can get muddied, lack horse sense, and become exposed to the truth in the most embarrassing ways is the instant we can see and realize that our reality has always been there. We indeed err in our judgments of situations. Still, a review is not what is called for in our self-realization—love is, acceptance is, and, most importantly, the expression of the acceptance of our love for ourselves and others is. If we believe we fail, we fail to believe in our success. We know our truth and express Truth, Love, Light, and Joy; we are the divine expressions of God, Spirit, the Cosmos, by whatever higher power you know as your truth and light we are, and we declare this perfection so.

In *Living the Science of Mind*, Holmes notes, "For just as there is an energy caught from the Universe and locked into the physical atom that can be loosed, so there is a spiritual energy caught in every person's mind and locked up in the individual life waiting to be used." In realizing this within ourselves, we release the atoms of our existence into positivity and fullest expression. We declare for ourselves the truth of our being, here and now.

To give thanks for the difficulty, to be grateful for the endlessly painful moments, this gratitude comes about in hindsight. To appreciate what cannot be tolerated, to find a gift in the muck and the mire, and to still be able to dance on a distant shoreline in a place so far away in the past of our lives, is blessed. While I look at these moments and wonder where in this decomposition of my life was that rationalization of truth, something more profound had come forward. It was all compost for the garden I had planted to bring forward the bounty of my desires. I am so happy to be where I am today. I am joyous in knowing that each day is another chance to stumble and to then turn it into a swiftly fantastic-looking dance move, or maybe see the light in someone who cannot see it for themselves, or better yet, clean up my act to follow a path to happiness.

A Prayer of Thanksgiving

If this prayer speaks to you, please feel free to use it in your daily practice. If you want to change this prayer to assist you in writing your own prayer, I support you in your discovery and welcome your creativity.

The purpose of this prayer is to give thanks for all of the gifts Life has given me.

RECOGNITION: The winds aloft move the weather in and out of the atmosphere, changing the clouds, bringing rain or snow, warmth or cold. The air has its pace, fast over the mountains, slower across the desert. The movement of the weather is the movement of Spirit through my life, effortlessly changing everything around me into a single breath filled with joy.

UNIFICATION: In the reciprocation of the breath, within me and around me, God and I are One. In that Oneness, all that moves within me and around me is inseparable, whole, perfect, and complete. Spirit is and I am, together as One I know this and express this in the gifts I have received and the gratitude I have been blessed with now.

My Life as Prayer

REALIZATION: All is ever-present in my life, and I am grateful for every step, every moment, and every Divine expression shown to me, given to me, and graced on me. I move effortlessly past obstacles toward my greater Good. I declare and affirm in this moment now that all is well and all is Good.

THANKSGIVING: It is with great gratitude that my abundance and joy in this life are manifested fully and completely. The gifts I have received in the knowledge and kindness of others, the prayers and abundance assuring my Good are infinite, filling me with love, light, and joy. The blessings of a life lived with lessons and light on my path to becoming a practitioner are many, and I give thanks for all I have received.

RELEASE: As I release my word into the Law, the blessings of Spirit manifest infinitely and abundantly, and so it is. Amen.

Chapter 5

Where to From Here?

Release: Set the Prayer Free

It is ready to become molded into any or all forms.
It is unexpressed Power, Substance, and Creativeness.
It is unexpressed Mind. It waits to be called into form
or expression. It exists in its original state, invisible but
potential with all possible form. A creative, universal energy
waiting to be used, to be operated upon. Willing,
but having no volition of Its own. Ready,
but having no initiative. Formless, but ready to take form.

— Ernest Holmes, *The Science of Mind*, pg. 392

Learning to Let Go

When I release my word, the spoken or written words of the affirmative prayer I know for another or myself is allowed to manifest and become the perfection it is, as this or something better. All that has been recognized as Spirit, unified in Spirit, realized in truth, and thanked for being as It is is returned to the flow of Life. It cannot be held or packaged into something else; it must be allowed to return from where it came to amplify all of the good and energies of Spirit. It is in the letting go that the blessing comes forward.

Today, this book is a a gift to my Sacred Soul Sisters who I graduated with in May 2022. In the last two years, during the COVID-19 pandemic, we have only been able to see each other in quick instances at church or, this last year, in our in-person classes. We were little boxes on the Zoom meeting platform on our laptops, tablets, and desktops at home. We loved and accepted each other, with no agendas, no sexual identifications required, no secret handshakes, no voodoo rites. There was nothing but Presence in our weekly gatherings.

COVID-19 changed so much of the world that what I knew of it two years ago, twenty years ago, and forty years ago became memories of my life that I bought into this element as a fascinating journey of self-discovery and reinvention, finding mastery in everything. I revel in my friendship with these beautiful light beings, my Sacred Soul Sisters, and I am in awe of who they are as they are. We were given a lovely Facebook group setting to follow each other's progress and holdups, life celebrations, and losses.

Whenever I could, I gave my gift to them in stories, thoughts on homework, and sneak peeks into my journaled thoughts. Some of them were my prayer partners in what looked like a darkened ordeal facing humanity, and all of them were my reason to keep going when it seemed things had stalled or were not going in the direction I thought things should. They are the rock I hold on to when the waves are crashing down. When something comes out of nowhere and disturbs me, they take me in; and when I make a mess out of myself, they love me enough to let me know I am still just fine by them.

Now we near the point of departure, and I am reminded of a moment leaving my military training to visit my family before I headed off to my first duty station. I am reminded of another group of women I admired, and they, too, stood with me through my trials and successes.

Flashback to 1984

For four months in the Alabama sun, in the summer of 1984, I was formed into a soldier and a military police officer. I was part of an all-female platoon, the second one assigned to this training brigade. The military had just let women into regular units fewer than eight years before, when President Gerald Ford signed into law an Act of Congress that took effect in 1976, disbanding the Women's Army Corps and other female-only units in the Navy, Marines, and Air Force, moving everyone into the regular military ranks. The military police was one of the few assignments where men and women were to train together, as the mission would require both to operate entirely without regard to gender.

Eight years in military terms is barely a blink of an eye, let alone a single synapse of response in the brain. We started as a group of thirty-six recruits. Most of us were "slick sleeves," private E-1; one or two were given a single chevron, private E-2, for some college work they may have done; and one was given private first-class status, E-3, for having an associate's degree.

I did not get an E-2 going in. That's how bad my grades were coming out of college. Within two weeks, we were down to twenty-eight women, either due to injuries that held them back in training further or discharged for behavior. One went absent without leave and was never found, which profoundly affected many of us. By the time we moved from the essential part of our training to the police side of our training, we were down to twenty regular Army personnel and six reservists who were brought in to complete their respective training. At the end of the training, sixteen soldiers graduated, thirteen as regular Army MPs and three as Army Reserve MPs. I was ranked eighth in the platoon, despite my drill sergeant being convinced I was too small to be of any value and too smart to be helpful as an enlisted soldier.

I was handed my military police diploma and a set of airline tickets for my flight out of Atlanta to D.C. The other tickets were to take me from D.C. to Los Angeles, Los Angeles to Honolulu. The drill sergeant gave me a glare and a firm warning not to screw up. Even though his eyes were misting up because I was the one buck private he couldn't muster out of the platoon, the drill sergeant shook my hand and then pushed me up onto the bus.

The Journey Begins

We got off at the main terminal. It was surreal. We looked at each other and did not know who the other was, forgetting our femininity and our first names. Knowing this was probably the last time we would ever see each other, we wanted to say our first names at least so the other would know it and recognize who we were in these heavy gabardine slacks, wool blazers, and heavy black berets with the giant brass Army logo mounted in them. We each stared at the other for a quick moment, and then one girl said

My Life as Prayer

she had to run for her flight to Denver; literally, she ran. The rest of us walked up to the security checkpoint, which wasn't much at the time. There were just two lanes open, and the personnel appeared bored out of their wits. The security officer saw us and flagged us through. We walked around the lines and kept going to wherever we were heading.

Two of the other girls split off, and we hugged briefly; their flights were to Louisville, Kentucky, and Rochester, New York. We had to be careful with our hugs and our goodbyes. We were frightened of who may be looking and who would think something of it. It was at a time when things were so misconstrued, especially in that part of the country in the early to mid-1980s, when AIDS and equal rights invoked hotbeds of anger in the southern United States. None of us could relax and be ourselves. We had no idea who was watching and from where.

The other soldier and I headed off in the other direction to our flights. As we came up to the escalator, she said, "We still don't know their names, but I want you to know who I am, OK? I may never see you again, but at least you know who I am, and please remember me if you do." She started to cry, and so did I. She grabbed my sleeve at the top of the escalator, looked right at me, then said goodbye, running to her gate, heading for Danville, Virginia, via Charlotte, North Carolina.

I stood there alone with my tears, filled with emotions I had not been allowed to express the whole time in training. The last friend I had in the group disappeared in the airport crowd. My flight wasn't going to leave for another hour, and it was a long walk to that gate. I had to let go. I had to focus on what was ahead of me now in my life. There was no one else going my way as I took the mobile walkway to the farthest end of the airport.

I released, let go, let whatever was ahead of me move me to that which serves me best, and I needed prayer now.

Chapter 5

Reflection

You have to let the prayer go, like letting doves fly out during a ceremony or balloons to commemorate someone's memory. It's the same as being a kid on the jungle gym at school or the neighborhood playground; you couldn't hold on to the rings or the monkey bars all day because, at some point, you had to let go. You had to move on so the other kids could play too or to go home for lunch or dinner. We all need to let go. No matter how hard it seems, no matter how beautiful and enthralling the prayer is, it must be released into Law.

In knowing all that I do now, my life, all life, is a prayer. As a practitioner of Religious Science, my prayer is five steps, and it lives within the feeling of the prayer to be held. The essential part of the prayer is the feeling—love, pleasure, comfort, and movement of joy. It is so powerful to feel those things that to release them is the ultimate freedom.

Yes, there are times when we may not have such an excellent feel for things. Loss is not easy—ever. Sadness creeps in where happiness leaves a void. Just when you think grief is a villain to every emotion that you felt was stolen from you, grief was mistaken for that chance to see that what matters are the legacies of love left behind. Grief asks you to share a legacy with the living. It does not ask you to take from it the void of love but to fulfill the promises you held in your heart for those moments that have past. Allow the feelings to come forward and allow the goodness of the words that spring from your heart to be heard.

Allow and release that which must be reciprocated infinitely, to manifest abundantly, that which is the good pleasure of the Lord. Let it all go and let God.

A Prayer of Release

If this prayer speaks to you, please feel free to use it in your daily practice. If you want to change this prayer to assist you in writing

My Life as Prayer

your own prayer, I support you in your discovery and welcome your creativity.

The purpose of this prayer is to let go and let God.

RECOGNITION: The snow releases from the mountaintops, melting down the sides of the avalanche chutes and cliffs. Every drop of water becomes destined, in its own way, to become a part of the earth or to wash alongside the rocks that lead to creeks, rivers, bays, and oceans. What had been snow, turned to water, is turned into the clouds above, nourishing and bringing forward the snow again. This reciprocation of Life is also the demonstration of nature's diversity in becoming what It is, to be the Wholeness just as the snow becomes the water and the water becomes the clouds. The water is ever-present and remains in the Oneness, no matter the form it takes.

UNIFICATION: In this Oneness is the union of all things, all nature, all Life. I am whole and present in knowing that as a child of God, wholeness is always present as Spirit and I are One, as One, through One. As I know this for myself, I am fulfilled in my union with Spirit. Like the water, I am whole in Oneness, no matter the form I take or become.

REALIZATION: As the water transitions into its many forms, I become that which I am, and I move through my life with ease and grace. As each era comes and goes in my world, I let go, and I let God. I am bringing forward the Light in my life, the expression of joy each day, and the truth of the love I feel each and every moment. I declare at this moment now that I let go of the things that do not serve me and allow Spirit to move me to where I need to be, what I need to become, and who I need to express, just as I am, effortlessly and completely.

Chapter 5

THANKSGIVING: To have the blessings I receive now is precious, and knowing that all is well and all is God fills my heart with gratitude and good. I give great thanks for this life I live and all that has been given to me.

RELEASE: As I release my word into the Law, knowing this prayer is manifesting infinitely and abundantly, fulfilled in its expression now, I let it go and I let God. And so it is. Amen.

As It passes into our being, It automatically becomes the law of our lives. It can pass into expression through us only as we consciously allow It to do so. Therefore, we should have faith in It, and Its desires, and Its ability to do for us all that we shall ever need to have done.

— Ernest Holmes, *The Science of Mind*, pg. 46

References

Holmes, E. 2009. *Creative Ideas,* Golden, Colorado: Science of Mind Publishing.

Holmes, E. 1984. *Living the Science of Mind,* Caramillo, California: DeVorss & Co.

Holmes, E. 1938. *The Science of Mind*. New York: Tarcherperigee.

About the Author

Joanie McMenamin, R.Sc.P, is a member of Mile Hi Church in Lakewood, Colorado, and a student of the teachings of Religious Science, founded by Ernest Holmes. Joanie is a graduate of practitioner studies through Centers for Spiritual Living and a licensed prayer practitioner. She has been an electro-mechanical inspector and technician for more than thirty years. She is an animal reiki practitioner and has three cats that enjoy her healing energy services. This book, her debut as an author, reflects her thoughts on life, Spirit, and other messy things.

Notes

Notes

Notes

Notes

Made in the USA
Columbia, SC
19 November 2023